What Was the Titanic?

by Stephanie Sabol

illustrated by Gregory Copeland

Penguin Workshop

For my sister Tina—SS

For my unsinkable mom, with love—GC

PENGUIN WORKSHOP
An Imprint of Penguin Random House LLC, New York

Visit us online at www.penguinrandomhouse.com.

Library of Congress Control Number: 2017052873

ISBN 9780515157260 (paperback)   20 19 18 17 16 15 14 13
ISBN 9780515157284 (library binding)   10 9 8 7 6 5 4 3 2

Contents

What Was the *Titanic*?

April 14, 1912

The grandest luxury ship ever, the *Titanic*, was crossing the Atlantic Ocean. It was on its maiden, or first, voyage. The ship had left England four days earlier. It was making great time. In just a few days, the *Titanic* was scheduled to arrive in New York City.

Aboard ship, the evening of April 14 seemed just like any other. First-class passengers enjoyed a feast with ten courses, including oysters and filet mignon. The *Titanic*'s captain, Edward John Smith, joined a dinner party in first class. It was hosted by a wealthy couple from Philadelphia.

After dinner, some first-class passengers played cards or listened to the orchestra. In second class, a minister sang hymns with about one hundred people. Down in third class, passengers danced together in their lounge, known as the general room. But after a long day at sea, many aboard the *Titanic* were already in bed.

Captain Smith checked in with his officers at the bridge around 9:00 p.m. The bridge was the command center of the ship. Smith told his officers to let him know if any problem arose. Then he went to his cabin.

Outside, the night was very cold. There was no moon, but the sky was clear. Thousands of stars shone brightly. The sea was so calm it looked like a mirror. No waves rippled in the distance.

Up in the crow's nest, two lookouts kept watch, ready to spot danger. In this part of the Atlantic, ice was a concern. Ships had to be very careful to avoid hitting an iceberg. The two lookouts chatted and tried to keep warm.

Then suddenly, at 11:40 p.m., almost out of nowhere, a large black shape came into view.

Could it be . . . ?

Yes, it was an iceberg!

The iceberg was almost directly ahead of the ship. It looked like the ship might run straight into it! The lookouts rang the warning bell three times—the signal for an emergency. They

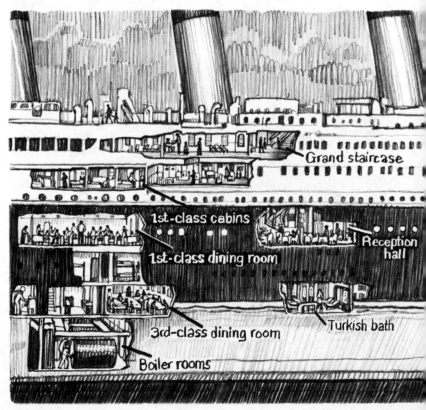

Grand staircase

1st-class cabins

Reception hall

1st-class dining room

3rd-class dining room

Turkish bath

Boiler rooms

telephoned the bridge where the officers were stationed. "Iceberg, right ahead!" they shouted.

The officers only had thirty-seven seconds to respond. First Officer William Murdoch contacted the engine room and ordered the ship's engines stopped and put into reverse. Would the *Titanic* avoid the iceberg? Or was it too late?

CHAPTER 1
The Age of Steam

Until the mid-1700s, ships had sails and relied on the power of the wind to move. Because winds are unpredictable, it wasn't possible to know exactly how long a trip would take. A ship might cross the Atlantic Ocean in either a few weeks or a few months.

By the early 1800s, steam engines began to power ships instead of sails. These steamships could cross the Atlantic in only two to four weeks.

Eventually, more powerful engines were built. A steamship with a powerful engine could cross the ocean in just ten to fourteen days.

Steamships grew in size over the years. They became known as ocean liners because they traveled the same route, or "line," regularly. These lines were like invisible roads across the ocean.

For rich passengers, crossing the Atlantic on an ocean liner was like being on a vacation. They enjoyed fine meals and luxurious cabins. For poor immigrants in the tight quarters of third class, the voyage offered the chance to leave their home countries and start new lives in the United States.

Millions of immigrants came to America from Europe during the late 1800s and early 1900s on enormous steamships.

At the end of the nineteenth century, two British shipping companies—the White Star Line and the Cunard Line—were in fierce competition with each other. In 1907, Cunard completed two ocean liners that could cross the Atlantic in only five days! How could the White Star Line show up Cunard? They couldn't make a faster ship. That wasn't possible. But could they make a bigger one?

CHAPTER 2
Building the *Titanic*

The White Star Line decided to build three new ships. One would be named the *Titanic*. (The names of all White Star Line ships ended in "ic.") Hundreds of blueprints and drawings were made. These plans would guide the workers during construction.

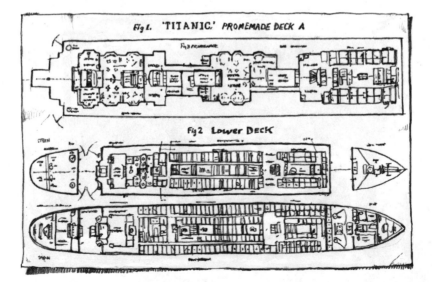

The Shipyard

The *Titanic* was going to be so big that a single slip (a ramp where ships are constructed) couldn't provide enough space. So three slips were turned into two. Then a giant metal gantry was built over the slip. A gantry is a bridge-like structure that supports equipment, such as cranes. This gantry was the largest in the world—almost one and a half times the length of a football field and as high as a nineteen-story building!

In March 1909, construction began at a huge shipyard in Belfast, Northern Ireland. Ships are built from the bottom up. First came the keel, which serves as the backbone of the ship and lies on its bottom. The keel is made of steel and supports the rest of the ship.

After the keel was made, curved steel beams joined the keel to form a U-shaped frame. The upper decks of the ship would eventually be built on the top of the beams. The framing of the

Titanic took about a year and was completed in April 1910.

Building the hull came next. The hull is the lower part of the ship that sits partly below water. It helps keep the ship afloat.

It took about six months to finish the hull. First, thousands of large sheets of steel were cut and shaped into plates. Some plates were flat, and some were curved. The plates were lined up side by side, with their edges overlapping. Then rivets—large iron tacks—were heated and inserted into holes in the steel plates. More than three million rivets were used on the *Titanic*.

The hull was divided into sixteen separate compartments. Walls called bulkheads separated them. If for any reason the ship started flooding, watertight doors in the bulkheads would instantly shut. The flooded compartments would be blocked off from one another. The *Titanic* could stay afloat even if the first four compartments filled with water. And it was hard to imagine any accident that would cause more flooding than that. Because of this, the newspapers called the *Titanic* "unsinkable." They didn't say "almost unsinkable." They said "unsinkable."

Who built the *Titanic*? Over fifteen thousand Irish shipyard workers. It was a grueling job. They worked Monday to Saturday from 6:00 a.m. to 5:30 p.m. They had a ten-minute break in the morning and a half hour off for lunch. It was dangerous work. Eight men died during the ship's construction.

On May 31, 1911, the hull of the *Titanic* was ready to be launched into the River Lagan. The black-painted hull now had the upper deck and four smokestacks but was empty inside. The launch would show whether the ship could stay afloat.

Launching an ocean liner was a big event. It was exciting to see a giant, freshly painted hull pulled down a ramp into the water for the first time.

Nearly one hundred thousand people gathered to see the *Titanic*'s launch. J. Bruce Ismay, director of the White Star Line, watched from a special grandstand. Wealthy American businessman J. P. Morgan was also there. His company owned the White Star Line.

When it was time, two bright red rockets exploded. This was to warn ships in the river to stay away from the launch site. It took sixty-two seconds for the hull to slide off its wooden platforms into the water.

Yes! The *Titanic* was seaworthy.

The workmen waved their hats, and the crowd cheered. Because the *Titanic* had no engine yet, smaller boats towed it up the river for a few minutes. Big anchors and cables prevented the ship from floating away. Then tugboats brought the *Titanic* back to the shipyard.

Now it was time to work on the inside—to turn the shell of the *Titanic* into a palace on the seas.

CHAPTER 3
Fitting Out the Ship

"Fitting out" a ship means putting in everything a ship needs, both to carry passengers and to power the vessel. Fitting out the *Titanic* took ten months.

Installing twenty-nine massive boilers was one of the first jobs. The boilers contained furnaces for coal that would be shoveled in to create fires. The fire would heat the water in the top of the boilers and turn it into steam. The steam would then travel through steel pipes to the engines.

The upper decks were constructed and painted, ten in all. Staircases between decks were built.

The grand staircase in first class was a

showstopper. It had oak paneling, carved railings, and an expensive clock. A glass dome high above the grand staircase let light stream in.

Hundreds of miles of electrical wiring were installed. Two thousand portholes (windows) were put in. Three giant funnels removed the smoke and fumes created by the coal fires in the boilers. Without funnels, soot would cover the passengers. The *Titanic* only needed three funnels. But the head builder thought four funnels would make the ship look grander. The fourth funnel was a fake!

In early February 1912, *Titanic's* three propellers were installed at the stern of the ship—two outside and one in the middle. Steam from the engines was fed through pipes to the propellers and made their blades turn. This caused the ship to move.

Ship Vocabulary

Sea travel has its own language. Here are some words to know:

Bow: front of a ship

Stern: back of a ship

Port: refers to the left side of the boat when standing at the rear and looking forward

Starboard: refers to the right side of the boat when standing at the rear and looking forward

Bridge: room from where the ship is commanded

Helm: the steering gear of a ship; the helm includes the wheel

Nautical mile: a unit used to measure distances at sea; it's equal to about 6,076 feet—that's almost eight hundred feet longer than a regular mile

Knot: a unit of speed equal to one nautical mile per hour

At top speed, *Titanic* could travel twenty-four knots (over twenty-seven miles per hour). That wasn't quite as fast as the *Lusitania*—a Cunard ship. But the *Titanic* was about more than speed— it was about luxury.

On April 2, 1912, *Titanic* had its sea trials. No tugboats pulled it. *Titanic* now ran on its own power. Captain Smith and his officers were on board. The crew practiced turns. They tested an emergency stop.

The sea trial went without a hitch.

After three years of construction, the *Titanic* was finally ready for its maiden voyage.

CHAPTER 4
Stuff and More Stuff

April 10, 1912 was the big day. The *Titanic* was set to depart from Southampton, England. But before any passengers could board, the cargo needed to be loaded.

Cargo included luggage and personal items belonging to passengers. One first-class family, the Ryersons, had sixteen large trunks! A fancy red

French car belonged to William Carter, who was returning home to Philadelphia with his family and servants. One of the most expensive items was a rare book of eleventh-century poems called

The Rubáiyát. Its cover was studded with over one thousand jewels— rubies, amethysts, and emeralds. The book had just been sold at an auction and was on its way to its new owner in New York.

The *Titanic* also carried commercial cargo— items that businesses sell. In 1912, the fastest way for companies in the United States to get goods from Europe was by passenger ship. *Titanic* had plenty of space to transport commercial goods, storing them in the lower decks. White Star Line could charge these companies a lot of money.

Commercial cargo included things like fabrics, food, cosmetic products, and seventy-six cases of a red dye called "dragon's blood."

Once the *Titanic* began its journey across the Atlantic, no food could be brought to it. Everything needed to feed approximately 2,200 people (a crew of nine hundred plus 1,300 passengers) already had to be on board. Seventy-five thousand pounds of fresh meat, forty thousand eggs, ten thousand pounds of sugar, and sixteen thousand lemons were only a small portion of the total food stored in the *Titanic*!

The full name of
the ship was RMS
Titanic. The RMS
stood for Royal Mail
Ship. *Titanic* was
to carry mail and
parcels across the
Atlantic for Great
Britain's postal service. There were nearly 3,500
sacks containing seven million pieces of mail!

Once the cargo was loaded, the crew came
on board. The head of the ship was Captain

Smith. All the crew obeyed
his orders. This was to be
Smith's last voyage. After
thirty-eight years working
for the White Star Line,
Captain Smith was ready
to retire.

The chief responsibility

Captain Smith

for Smith and his seven officers was to keep the ship on course, issuing orders to the engine room. The engineering crew had a dirty job in the noisy bottom of the ship. Twenty-five engineers and 176 stokers worked around the clock to keep the boiler full of coal and the engines running.

Smith and his officers also supervised the deck crew. The deck crew was in charge of the day-to-day running of the ship. There were carpenters, lookouts, store clerks, window cleaners, and quartermasters. A quartermaster's job is to look after supplies. The deck crew also included twenty-nine seamen who were trained to operate the twenty lifeboats. Of course, no one imagined they'd need to be used.

And then there was the "victualling crew." This crew of over three hundred people took care of the passengers. They included waitstaff, maids, and attendants. They served food, made beds, and saw to the passengers' everyday needs. The kitchen crew was so big that there were cooks who only made fish dishes; others who only prepared vegetables. There were even cooks who just prepared sauces or soups.

Last to board were the passengers. Thomas Andrews, the ship's architect, was the very first.

Thomas Andrews

He wanted to make sure the voyage went smoothly. J. Bruce Ismay was among the first passengers to board. He had a fancy parlor suite with a private deck.

Over 1,300 passengers walked up the gangways. Musicians, high on the upper decks, played in celebration. Soon the passengers on board were waving to the crowd cheering from the dock. The *Titanic* blew its whistle, and it was off to sea.

From Southampton, England, the *Titanic* proceeded to Cherbourg, France, four hours away. About three hundred more passengers came on board while several got off. Then the *Titanic* traveled overnight to Queenstown, Ireland. Over one hundred new passengers and more mail boarded the *Titanic*.

Around 1:40 p.m. on April 11, the ship finally set out for New York. The *Titanic*'s whistle gave three long and deep blasts. A small boat replied with a short honk, and the *Titanic* let out one final blast. It was the last time the *Titanic* would see land.

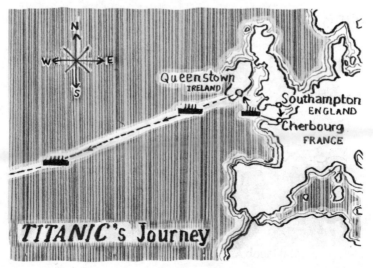

TITANIC's Journey

CHAPTER 5
Life aboard the Ship

Titanic's passengers came from over thirty countries—some as far away as Thailand and Uruguay. However, most passengers were from Great Britain and the United States.

Most of the top four decks were for first-class passengers. The most expensive suite cost over $60,000 in today's money! Forty-seven-year-old John Jacob Astor IV of New York City was the

John Jacob Astor IV and his wife, Madeleine

richest passenger on board. The Astor family had made their money in fur trading and owning lots of land. Astor and his wife, Madeleine, were traveling home to New York City after their honeymoon. Another first-class passenger, Margaret Tobin Brown (known as Molly Brown), had been married to a Denver mining tycoon. Isidor Straus, the co-owner of Macy's department store in New York City, traveled with his wife, Ida. They had been on vacation in Europe.

Molly Brown

Staying in the first-class cabins was like staying in a luxurious floating hotel. Some came with sitting rooms and small sleeping rooms for maids. Not all first-class cabins were alike—some were decorated with fancy French furniture while others looked like rooms from an English mansion.

Some had fireplaces and ornate moldings and light fixtures. White Star Line advertised the splendor of first class: "It is impossible to . . . describe the decorations in the passenger accommodation. . . . They are on a scale of . . . magnificence. Nothing like them has ever appeared before on the ocean."

The second-class cabins were clean and well lit. Most had bunk beds, a sofa, and a desk. In fact, *Titanic*'s second class was just as nice as many other ships' first class. Cabins slept two to four people. Twelve-year-old Ruth Becker was traveling with her mother and two siblings in second class.

She said, "Everything was new. New! . . . Our cabin was just like a hotel room, it was so big."

Most passengers were in third class, in the lowest decks. Third-class cabins were plain. Most had four beds, an electric light, and a small sink. (To have running water in third class was very unusual.) The seven hundred people traveling in third class had to share just two bathtubs! Most passengers didn't mind too much. After all, they would be arriving in New York soon. And they were getting there on the most famous ship in the world—the *Titanic*.

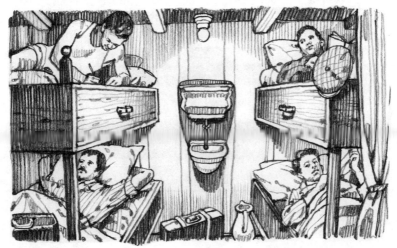

The Passenger List

Exact numbers aren't known. There might have been last-minute changes to the passenger list before *Titanic* set sail. But the approximate breakdown was as follows:

First-Class Passengers: 329

Second-Class Passengers: 285

Third-Class Passengers: 710

Crew: 899

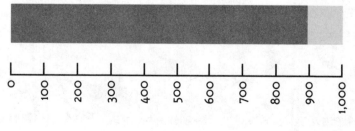

What did people do all day?

First-class passengers had many choices. Perhaps they would try out the machines in the gymnasium—a stationary bike or rowing machine—or relax in the steam of the Turkish bath. The Turkish bath had beautiful mosaic tiles with a Moorish (North African) theme. There were golden beams and bronze lamps. People lounged on comfortable chairs after they took a steam bath.

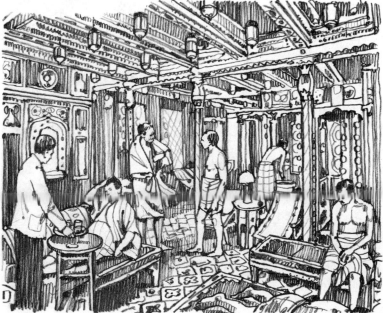

There was also a pool filled with seawater. Boilers warmed the water to room temperature. The only other ship that had a swimming pool at that time was *Titanic*'s sister ship, *Olympic*. The pool was reserved for first-class passengers only, and they had to pay twenty-five cents for a ticket!

Second-class passengers had their own library and smoking room. They played cards, chess, or dominoes. They could stroll on the promenade deck reserved for second class. (*Promenade* means walkway.)

In third class, passengers held dances in the general room. They were able to take walks or play games on the poop deck (the high deck at the stern of the ship). Ten-year-old Frank Goldsmith and a few other boys from third class found their way to the lower decks and waved hello to the firemen and stokers.

Nothing beat the food on the *Titanic*. First-class passengers ate in a beautiful saloon with expensive oak furniture. It was the largest dining

saloon on any ship at the time. The tiled floor
was designed to look like a Persian carpet. Waiters
served passengers lobster and caviar from sterling
silver platters. The Café Parisien was a popular
eating spot for younger first-class passengers. It
looked like a sidewalk café in Paris.

First class was fanciest in every way, but being in second class was still very pleasant. The dining room was filled with mahogany furniture with dark red upholstery. There was also a piano.

Third class had its own dining room, too, although much plainer. Even so, having a third-class dining room was very unusual. On other ships, third-class passengers had to bring their own food for the entire trip and cook it themselves.

CHAPTER 6
Warnings

While the passengers were enjoying themselves, J. Bruce Ismay paid close attention to the clock. The trip was supposed to take eight days. But he wanted the *Titanic* to get to New York sooner. An early arrival in New York would be great publicity for the White Star Line.

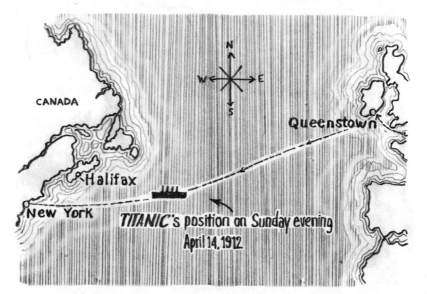

TITANIC's position on Sunday evening April 14, 1912

How Did the *Titanic* Communicate
with Other Ships?

Before the telegraph was invented, ships had to rely on flags or light signals from nearby ships to warn of dangers ahead.

In 1901, Italian engineer Guglielmo Marconi invented the wireless radio telegraph. The telegraph used radio waves to send messages through the air. The *Titanic*'s operators used Morse code, a system of dots and dashes, to communicate messages. These messages were sent to and from other ships or to stations on land.

By Sunday night, April 14, the *Titanic* was two-thirds of the way to New York. *Titanic*'s two radio operators worked in their small office, sending and receiving messages by telegraph. Most were communications with nearby ships.

The operators were very busy. The telegraph had stopped working for several hours the night before. Because of this, they now had a bottleneck of messages to send—many were personal ones from passengers to family and friends at home. However, the operators' main job was to learn about any possible dangers ahead.

After four days of steady travel, the *Titanic* had entered an ice field. On April 14, the radio operators received seven ice warnings from nearby ships. One ice warning came mid-afternoon from the *Baltic* and warned of large icebergs about 250 miles away. The operators passed the message to Captain Smith. He decided to alter the course of the ship slightly and travel ten miles farther south than usual. He believed that would be enough of a change to avoid any serious ice.

Were the captain and officers alarmed? It didn't seem so. The ship was so well built, perhaps Captain Smith believed it was unsinkable. He never told his officers to slow down the speed of the ship. The *Titanic* was traveling "full steam ahead."

That night the air temperature began to drop. Passengers felt the chill in the air. Wealthy ladies wrapped themselves in fur. Most people were content to stay indoors instead of walking the decks. There was no moon out and nothing to see but blackness.

At 10:55 p.m., the radio operators received the last ice warning of the day. Later on, a nearby ship, the *Californian*, tried to alert the *Titanic* to danger ahead. But *Titanic*'s operator was too busy sending messages from passengers. He dismissed the message and told *Californian*'s radio operator to "shut up"!

Icebergs

An iceberg is an enormous piece of ice that has broken off from a glacier or an ice sheet. Ocean currents and tides slowly carry an iceberg out to sea. The iceberg that hit the *Titanic* began forming on the west coast of Greenland around fifteen thousand years earlier. It was likely four hundred feet long.

Only about 10 percent of an iceberg's mass can be seen. The rest is underneath the water's surface.

Forty-five minutes after the *Californian's* warning, *Titanic's* two lookouts were keeping watch during the cold, clear night. It had been quiet since they took their post at 10:00 p.m. But the calm was about to end.

At 11:40 p.m. the lookouts spotted a large dark shape in the water. What could it be?

An iceberg!

Quickly they rang the alarm bell and reported that the *Titanic* was heading straight for an iceberg!

CHAPTER 7
Iceberg!

With seconds to react, First Officer Murdoch ordered the engines to be stopped, then reversed. Then he ordered the ship to turn to avoid hitting the iceberg head-on. But making a gigantic ocean liner turn is very hard. It can't swerve to avoid an accident like a car can.

First Officer Murdoch

The officers held their breath as the ship turned. It was too late. The side of the boat hit the berg, and the rivets (which held the steel plates of the hull together) popped out. Now it seemed there was a three-hundred-foot-long opening along the ship's starboard side.

Immediately, Captain Smith left his cabin and rushed to his officers. He had felt the collision. "What did we strike?" he asked. "An iceberg," Murdoch replied. Captain Smith appeared calm. First, he asked if the watertight doors that sealed off the hull compartments from one another were closed. He ordered the engines stopped, hoping to slow down any water that might flow into the ship. Then he asked another officer to check the bottom of the boat for damage.

The first report was good. The officer didn't see any damage. But he hadn't gone far enough down into the ship. Then came terrible news. The mail room was already flooding. Seven tons of water rushed in every second. Postal workers were scrambling to bring hundreds of mailbags to higher decks.

Captain Smith met with Thomas Andrews, the ship's architect. Andrews had just inspected the lower decks himself. In only ten minutes, the water in the bow had risen fourteen feet above the keel. The water couldn't be contained to just four compartments. And four was the maximum number that could be flooded with the *Titanic* still being able to stay afloat. Andrews gave the boat less than two hours before it sank.

The *Titanic* was doomed.

Five minutes after midnight, Captain Smith ordered his officers to uncover the lifeboats. *Titanic* was equipped with twenty lifeboats. But they could only hold 1,178 people. That meant over one thousand people would be left stranded aboard the *Titanic*.

Although some passengers had heard a loud noise when the ship hit the iceberg, many had slept through the collision. In first class, the crew kept calm as they knocked on cabin doors, urging passengers to put on life jackets and go to the top deck. Nothing was seriously wrong, they said. The captain was just being cautious.

In the lower decks of third class, the crew didn't bother being polite. They ran down the halls, yelling at passengers to put on life jackets immediately. Many passengers—even those who couldn't understand English—didn't need to be told. They could already see water pouring into the ship.

CHAPTER 8
Abandon Ship!

At 12:10 a.m. Captain Smith entered the wireless room. He told the operators to send the call for help. Immediately, they sent the Morse code distress signal: "CQD." A short while later, they tapped out "SOS," the brand-new international call for help. This was one of the first times in history "SOS" was used.

Three ships replied to the signal, the closest being the *Carpathia*. But it was fifty-eight miles away. How could it reach the *Titanic* in time? Even at its top speed, the *Carpathia* was about four hours away.

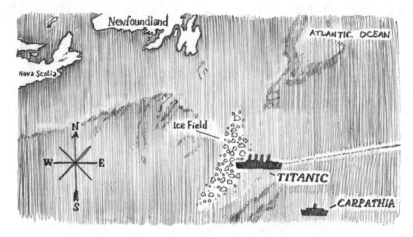

Passengers began to fill the outer decks of the ship. By this time, some could tell they were walking on a slight slope. Still, most didn't want to believe that anything so terrible had happened that lifeboats were needed. Indoors, the ship was warm and comfortable. Why risk getting into a tiny lifeboat on the cold, dark sea? Especially since the *Titanic* was supposed to be unsinkable. When the first lifeboat was lowered at 12:45 a.m., it was less than half full. Ten minutes later, officers launched the first of eight white distress flares into the sky. Each flare exploded with a loud bang. Would another ship see them?

First- and second-class passengers waited on the boat deck. Some were dressed in warmer clothes. The orchestra set themselves up and began playing cheerful music.

Downstairs in the lower decks, there was more confusion as third-class passengers ran down hall

after hall. They tried to find stairways that led to the top deck. However, it was like finding the way out of a maze. Many didn't speak English and couldn't read the signs. Hundreds of third-class passengers never made it to the deck where the lifeboats were.

As the bow of the ship kept sinking, the rest of the *Titanic* tilted higher and higher out of the water. Furniture was sliding across the decks. By now, it became clear that everyone needed to

get off the sinking ship—fast. But not everyone could, not with only twenty lifeboats. And there had never been a safety drill, either. Passengers didn't know what to do.

Ship Lifeboats

Titanic had over 2,200 people on board, but its twenty lifeboats only had room for 1,178 people. (There were sixteen regular lifeboats and four inflatable ones.) The White Star Line hadn't broken any laws, though. A boat the *Titanic*'s size was only required to have enough lifeboats for 962 people.

Most ship owners believed that in an emergency, another ship would be near enough to rescue everyone. The job of the lifeboats would be to take passengers from the ship in trouble to the rescue vessel. The lifeboats would serve as ferries, taking one group of passengers after another to safety. No one imagined a situation in which everyone would need to be evacuated on lifeboats, all at the same time.

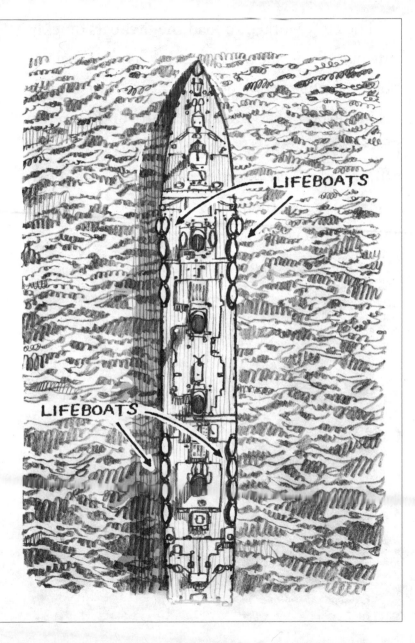

LIFEBOATS

LIFEBOATS

The crew worked to load the lifeboats quickly. But passengers started panicking as they realized not everyone would be saved. One officer shot his revolver in the air as a group of frightened passengers fought to get on a lifeboat. Another officer had the crew form a ring around a lifeboat. The men locked their arms together. Only women and children were allowed through.

According to all ships' rules, women and children were to get in the boats first. John Jacob Astor IV said goodbye to his wife, Madeleine. He tossed his gloves to her as the lifeboat was lowered. She would never see him again.

Isidor Strauss urged his wife, Ida, to get on a lifeboat. She refused. "We have lived together for many years. Where you go, I go."

Captain Smith dismissed the men in the wireless room. "You can do no more. Now it's every man for himself." That meant crew members should try to save themselves in whatever way they could.

As for Captain Smith, he didn't intend to go anywhere. He would go down with his ship. The *Titanic* was indeed his final voyage, but there would be no peaceful years of retirement for him.

At 2:05 a.m. the last lifeboat launched into the sea. Over 1,500 passengers remained on board, screaming in panic, grabbing railings to hold. Some people decided to jump into the frigid ocean, hoping to swim to safety.

It was now 2:18 a.m.

The whole bow of the ship was no longer visible and the stern rose nearly vertical toward

the sky. All the *Titanic's* lights went out. With a terrible sound, the ship snapped in two pieces and sank.

Only two hours and forty minutes after the *Titanic* hit the iceberg, it was gone.

One passenger in a lifeboat later wrote, "As the *Titanic* plunged deeper and deeper we could see her stern rising higher and higher until her lights began to go out. As the last lights on the stern went out we saw her plunge . . . Then the screams began and seemed to last eternally."

Only about seven hundred passengers had made it onto the lifeboats. They watched in horror. Some sat in silence. Others wailed. Many couldn't grasp what they were seeing. It all had happened so fast. One passenger said, "The sounds of people drowning are something that I cannot describe to you, and neither can anyone else. It's the most dreadful sound and there is a terrible silence that follows it."

Some passengers in the lifeboats wanted to row to those in the water and help them. But others were frightened that swimmers would overwhelm the lifeboats. In the end, only one lifeboat returned to try to save anybody. In the water, some held on to deck chairs as mini rafts. Even with life jackets, people couldn't stay alive for more than about twenty minutes in water that was only twenty-eight degrees.

Soon, the cries of those in the sea began to quiet. A woman in lifeboat number four watched shooting stars in the sky. She had never seen so many. She remembered a legend that said, every time you see a shooting star, somebody dies.

Now there was nothing for survivors to do but wait and hope for rescue. They were all alone on the cold, dark sea.

Timeline of Disaster

11:40 p.m.: The *Titanic* hits the iceberg

12:05 a.m.: Captain Smith orders the crew to uncover the lifeboats and alert passengers

12:15 a.m.: First wireless call for help

12:45 a.m.: First lifeboat lowered

2:05 a.m.: Last lifeboat lowered

2:10 a.m.: Last wireless call sent

2:18 a.m.: Lights go out on the ship

2:20 a.m.: The *Titanic* sinks

The RMS *Titanic*

Launch of the *Titanic* at Southampton, England, May 31, 1911

Propellers on the *Titanic*

Inspector examines lifejackets on the *Titanic* before its voyage, 1912

First-class lounge on the *Titanic*

Reading room

A private suite

Illustration of the first-class dining room

"Cycle racing machines" in the gymnasium

J. Bruce Ismay, the director of the White Star Line

Replica of the grand staircase

Survivors in one of the collapsible lifeboats

Survivors in a lifeboat picked up by the RMS *Carpathia*

The lifeboats that carried most of the 705 survivors

Survivors of the *Titanic* on the *Carpathia*

New York Times front page about the sinking

Newspaper boy on April 14, 1912

Titanic stewards waiting to be questioned about the sinking, 1912

US Senate hearing investigating the RMS *Titanic* sinking, 1912

Captain Arthur Rostron of the *Carpathia* with
Titanic survivor Molly Brown

The submersible *Argo* searching for the *Titanic* in 1985

Cynthia Johnson/The LIFE Images Collection/Getty Images

American oceanographer Robert Ballard announces
his discovery of the wreckage, 1985

Dishes from the *Titanic* on the ocean floor

CHAPTER 9
Rescue

Once the *Carpathia* received the *Titanic's* distress signal, Captain Arthur Henry Rostron went into action. He had the crew gather blankets and prepare hot drinks and soup. The three doctors on board each turned a dining room into a hospital. The gangway doors were opened and ropes and ladders were hung to transfer survivors from lifeboats to the ship.

The *Carpathia* sped as fast as she could in dangerous icy water. Every fifteen minutes, the *Carpathia* fired rockets and cannons in the air to show they were coming. Around 3:30 a.m. the ship arrived where the *Titanic* had sunk.

People in the lifeboats heard *Carpathia*'s cannons before they saw the ship. At 4:00 a.m. the first of the *Titanic*'s survivors were brought to safety. Women were lifted on board with sling chairs, while children were lifted up in canvas bags. Men climbed up ladders. For the next four hours, the *Carpathia* took on more than seven hundred passengers. They were freezing and in shock. Women already on board the *Carpathia* stood at the railing, watching the other lifeboats empty. They were hoping to see husbands, fathers, or children from whom they had been separated. Too often there was no happy reunion.

Some men, mostly from first class, had been in lifeboats. J. Bruce Ismay had been one of the

last to board one. When he reached the deck of the *Carpathia*, he looked dazed. He could barely speak. Ismay didn't respond to Captain Rostron's questions. Ismay sent a telegram to the White Star Line: "Deeply regret advise you *Titanic* sank this morning after collision with iceberg, resulting in serious loss of life. Full particulars later." Ismay stayed alone in a stateroom for the rest of the trip.

Joseph Bruce Ismay (1862–1937)

Joseph Bruce Ismay was the son of the founder of the White Star Line. After his father died in 1899, Ismay took over the company business. It was his idea to build the *Titanic* as the grandest ship on the sea.

Ismay stepped into the last lifeboat that left the *Titanic*. Many people felt it was cowardly of the head of the company to save himself while so many others died. His reputation would never recover. Ismay spent the rest of his life in seclusion—it is said that no one was allowed to speak of the *Titanic* in his presence. He died in 1937.

By the morning of April 15 in New York, London, and around the world, the terrible news was spreading. Other ships on the North Atlantic had sent messages to land. The information, however, was incomplete or wrong. The *Evening Sun* reported, "ALL SAVED FROM TITANIC AFTER COLLISION." The *New York Times* was much closer to the truth. Its headline read, "TITANIC SINKS FOUR HOURS AFTER HITTING ICEBERG [. . .] PROBABLY 1250 PERISH." A list of survivors was posted outside their offices.

Three days later, on April 18, the *Carpathia* slowly steamed into New York City's harbor. A crowd of nearly thirty thousand people waited at the Cunard pier (the *Carpathia* was a Cunard ship). But the ship crept past it and stopped at the nearby White Star Line pier. The onlookers were confused —why would a Cunard ship go there? Soon it became clear. Each of the *Titanic*'s empty lifeboats were lowered into the water at the White Star

Line pier. They were all that was left of the ship.

After the *Carpathia* returned to its own pier around 9:00 p.m., the first passengers walked down the gangway. When Ismay left the ship, he was met by two United States senators. They had an order for him to appear at an investigation of the disaster the next day. The world wanted to know why this tragedy had happened.

CHAPTER 10
The Lost

Over eight hundred passengers and nearly seven hundred crew members lost their lives in the *Titanic* disaster. Most of the passengers who died were from third class (about 540). Among the victims in first or second class, nearly all were men. Fifty-four victims were children—all except one was from third class.

Many of the crew had lived in Southampton, England. More than five hundred households lost at least one family member. At one school, the teacher asked all the children who had a relative on the *Titanic* to stand. Every child in the class rose.

What happened to the bodies of the dead? Two days after the disaster, White Star Line sent several ships looking for them. Three hundred twenty-

eight bodies were found. Some of them floated upright in the water, lifted by their life jackets. They looked like they were sleeping. Others were too hard to identify. They were buried at sea. John Jacob Astor IV was identified by the initials inside his collar. His body was covered in soot. It's likely he died when one of the funnels fell over and crushed him.

The bodies were taken to Halifax, Canada. Some were claimed by family members. The rest were buried in nearby cemeteries. Hundreds of bodies were never recovered. They were trapped within the ship at the bottom of the sea.

Around the world, people remained shocked by the disaster and the terrible loss of life. The *Titanic* was supposed to be unsinkable. How could such a tragedy have happened?

The US inquiry found that the crew had not been prepared for an emergency. The Senate blamed the British Board of Trade for having outdated rules about the number of lifeboats that ships were required to carry. They also believed that Captain Smith, perhaps spurred on by J. Bruce Ismay, went too fast in dangerously icy water. (The British inquiry did not blame Captain Smith.)

The Senate stated their recommendations. First, all ships were to have lifeboats for everyone on board. Crew members must be trained on how

to lower the lifeboats and properly row them. Ship crews were to have regular lifeboat drills for the passengers.

The Senate also recommended that all ships install wireless radios operating twenty-four hours a day. Not every ship used wireless radios when the *Titanic* sank. If the *Titanic* and the *Carpathia* hadn't both had them, there would have been no rescue. Many more lives would have been lost.

In 1914, Canada, the United States, and countries in Western Europe joined together to

start the International Ice Patrol (IIP). The patrol used boats (and later planes) to locate icebergs in the Atlantic and alert ships in the area.

Traveling by ship definitely became safer, but the great age of luxury liners was coming to an end.

Why?

There was a newer, much faster way to cross the ocean—in an airplane.

CHAPTER 11
Discovery

Shortly after the *Titanic* sank, people became interested in salvaging, or recovering, the sunken ship. There were two problems: First, no one knew exactly where the ship had sunk. After *Titanic* sent its final distress signal, the ship drifted with the ocean currents. The search area was over one hundred miles wide. The ocean in this area was two and a half miles deep. Second, even if the ship could be located, how could it be recovered? There were some crazy ideas—one was to fill the boat with Ping-Pong balls and float it to the surface! A Denver inventor published a plan to raise the *Titanic* using a submarine and powerful magnets.

By the 1980s, undersea technology had

advanced to the point where locating a ship—
even one so far below the surface—was possible.

Robert Ballard, an American underwater
archaeologist, had dreamed of finding the *Titanic*
for years. He figured out what kind of vehicle might
be able to locate the *Titanic*, and he developed a
submersible called *Argo*. *Argo* was fifteen feet long
and about three and a half feet high and wide.
It was unmanned—meaning there would be no

people inside. *Argo* was equipped with floodlights, video cameras, and a sonar system. Sonar uses sound waves to locate underwater objects. Once underwater, *Argo* was controlled by people on a boat above water. *Argo* could take pictures and send them back to the surface.

Robert Ballard (1942–)

Robert Ballard is one of the best-known deep-sea explorers. Born in 1942, Ballard grew up in San Diego, California. From an early age, he was interested in underwater exploration. Ballard worked as an oceanographer for the US Navy. He researched different technologies and developed a robotic vehicle to search for the *Titanic* underwater. In 1985, he put his invention to the test.

Although Ballard has explored many other shipwrecks, he is most well-known for his discovery of the *Titanic*.

In 1985, Ballard put together a team to find the wreck of the *Titanic*. American and French research scientists joined a ship called the *Knorr*, which searched the Atlantic for six weeks. But nothing turned up. The team was losing hope.

Then just after midnight on September 1, 1985, *Argo* detected something odd—small chunks of metal located at a depth of 12,500 feet (about two miles). On the *Knorr*, the team studied the video screens. These metal chunks looked human-made. *Argo* continued to send up images. Soon it located something enormous and circular. Could this be one of *Titanic*'s boilers? The team quickly checked an old photograph from 1911—

The boiler from the *Titanic* found underwater

it looked exactly the same! They cheered—they had found the *Titanic*!

Ballard and his team were thrilled. But their celebration took place at the spot where hundreds of people had lost their lives. A memorial service was held for all those who had died.

The next day, Ballard sent *Argo* underwater again. This time *Argo* located the bow of the ship. The steel was dark black and covered in rust. It looked like a skeleton of the once-grand ship.

Argo found the stern lying nearly two thousand feet away from the bow. This was an important discovery. People hadn't been sure whether the *Titanic* had sunk in one piece or had broken in two. *Argo* solved that mystery—the *Titanic* had indeed split in half.

People had also believed that the iceberg tore a three-hundred-foot gash in the side of the hull. Seeing the hull showed that was not so. There was no tear—the rivets had popped open under the pressure of hitting the iceberg.

The next summer, Ballard got ready for another trip to the wreck. And he planned to see it for himself. This time he would get into a tiny submarine called *Alvin*—and go over twelve

thousand feet underwater! Ballard stepped into *Alvin* with his handheld video camera. It took him two and a half hours to travel from the surface to the wreck. He would go on eleven dives in total.

So what did Ballard discover? Thousands of objects were found lying around the stern. They included portholes, dishes, and even a bathtub. Ballard did not take anything—he thought a grave site should be left alone. Instead, he and his team left two plaques. One was in memory of all who died. The other asked all future explorers to leave the ship in peace.

The plaque didn't stop professional treasure hunters in future explorations. Items from the *Titanic* were worth a lot of money. Some of the recovered artifacts included jewelry and luggage. A cherub statue from the grand staircase was found. A toy doll's porcelain head was found half buried in the seafloor.

Can the *Titanic* be raised? No. It's too fragile to move. Scientists have discovered that it is slowly being eaten by bacteria. The bacteria have created rusticles—long, icicle-like structures made of rust.

Some experts believe that the wreck will turn into dust within fifty years. There will be nothing left of the *Titanic*.

Titanic Mania

Even right after the disaster, the world wanted to know every detail about the tragic maiden voyage. Newspapers and magazines printed special editions just days after the ship sank. The first movie about the *Titanic* came out just one month later. It was called *Saved from the Titanic*. Actress Dorothy Gibson starred in the movie—she had actually been a first-class passenger! In the movie she wore the same clothes she'd worn on the *Titanic*.

A Night to Remember is one of the most popular books written about the disaster. The author, Walter Lord, interviewed over sixty survivors for his account. In 1958 the book was turned into a movie. The movie sets were made from actual *Titanic* blueprints.

The most expensive movie ever made about the disaster was the 1997 film *Titanic*. It cost $200 million to make. Director James Cameron made a

giant model ship—it was nearly the same size as the actual *Titanic*. The team used a seventeen-million-gallon water tank to film the sinking. The expensive price tag wound up not being a big deal—the movie earned more than $2 billion worldwide!

In 2017, workers in China started building a full-size replica of the *Titanic*—882½ feet long! Visitors will be able to eat on the ship and stay overnight. Luckily, there will be no chance of icebergs—the ship will stay docked in a reservoir.

CHAPTER 12
What If?

Perhaps the most tragic part of the *Titanic* story is that it could have been avoided. If only one thing had happened differently that night, there might never have been a disaster.

What if the lookouts had seen the iceberg sooner? The calm sea and moonless sky made it difficult to see anything on the water. If there had been waves that night, the lookouts might have spotted them splashing against the sixty-foot-tall iceberg. If there had been even a little bit of moonlight, it could have helped to point out the iceberg. And what if the lookouts had had their binoculars? They had been locked in a cupboard and nobody on board had the key!

Once the iceberg was spotted, Murdoch

ordered the ship to turn. But what if the *Titanic* had hit the berg head-on? Many think the damage wouldn't have been nearly as bad, and the *Titanic* would have remained afloat.

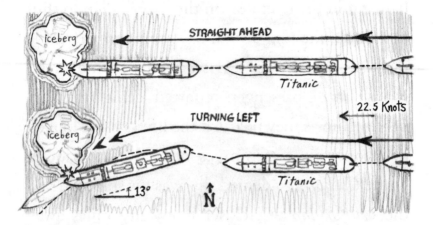

What if the ten-foot-high bulkheads between compartments had reached all the way to the very top of the deck? That might have contained the water rushing in. Instead, when each compartment filled with water, water immediately began spilling over into the next compartment—just like an ice cube tray. It didn't take very long before all the compartments in the front of the ship were flooded.

The what-ifs don't end there. What if Captain Smith had paid closer attention to the ice warnings and ignored Ismay's desire for the ship to keep going at top speed? What if the *Titanic's* radio operator hadn't told the operator on the *Californian* to shut up? Could the *Californian* have come to the rescue in time if it had known the *Titanic* was in distress? Many *Titanic* passengers reported seeing lights of a nearby ship as they boarded the lifeboats. It looked to be only five to ten miles away. But the captain of the *Californian* denied this was his ship. He said the *Californian* was closer to twenty miles away and never saw flares from the *Titanic*.

Most important of all, what if there had been enough lifeboats? The *Titanic* still would have sunk, but everyone—or nearly everyone—might have been saved. Captain Rostron of the *Carpathia* wrote, "It hardly bears thinking about that if there had been sufficient boats that night . . . every soul aboard could have been saved, since it was two and a half hours after she struck that she tilted her massive stern into the heavens and sank by the head, taking with her all that were unprovided for."

If only one of these things had happened differently, the night might not have ended so tragically. Instead, 1,500 lives were lost. More than a hundred years later, the sinking of the *Titanic* remains one of the greatest disasters at sea of all time.

Timeline of the Titanic

1845 — The White Star Line is founded in Liverpool, England

1909 — Construction of the *Titanic* begins at a shipyard in Northern Ireland

1912 — April 10: The *Titanic*'s maiden voyage sets sail from Southampton, England

— April 14: *Titanic* receives seven ice warnings from nearby ships in the North Atlantic Ocean

— April 15: *Titanic* sinks in the early morning

— April 18: The *Carpathia*, carrying *Titanic*'s survivors, arrives in New York City

— April 19: The US inquiry into the *Titanic* disaster begins

1914 — A Denver inventor publishes a plan to raise the *Titanic* using a submarine and powerful magnets

— The International Ice Patrol is formed

1937 — J. Bruce Ismay dies at age seventy-four

1955 — Walter Lord's *A Night to Remember* is published

1985 — Robert Ballard and team discover the wreck of the *Titanic*

1997 — *Titanic* movie releases worldwide; it goes on to earn $2 billion at the box office

2009 — The last known survivor of the *Titanic* passes away

Timeline of the World

1819 — The SS *Savannah* is the first steamship to cross the Atlantic Ocean

1901 — Guglielmo Marconi invents the wireless radio telegraph

1903 — Wright brothers make first powered airplane flight

1911 — First film studios open in Hollywood

1914 — Charlie Chaplin invents his Little Tramp character

— World War I begins

1915 — Almost 1,200 people die when the Cunard ship *Lusitania* is torpedoed by a German U-boat

1927 — Charles Lindbergh completes the first solo nonstop flight across the Atlantic Ocean in 33.5 hours

1937 — The *Hindenburg*, the largest airship ever, explodes before landing in New Jersey

1939 — World War II begins

1945 — A Soviet submarine sinks the *Wilhelm Gustloff*, resulting in over 9,000 deaths—the largest loss of life at sea

— World War II ends

1956 — Elvis Presley's first record, "Heartbreak Hotel," is released

1981 — Sandra Day O'Connor becomes the first woman on the Supreme Court

1997 — Princess Diana dies in a car crash in Paris

2009 — Barack H. Obama becomes the first black president of the United States

Bibliography

*Books for young readers

*Brewster, Hugh, and Laurie Coulter. *882 ½ Amazing Answers to Your Questions about the Titanic*. New York: Scholastic, 1998.

*Fullman, Joe. *The Story of Titanic for Children*. London: Carlton Kids, 2015.

*Hughes, Susan, and Steve Santini. *The Science and Story of Titanic*. Toronto: Somerville House, 1999.

Lord, Walter. *A Night to Remember*. New York: Holt, Rinehart & Winston, 1955.

Lynch, Don. *Titanic: An Illustrated History*. New York: Hyperion Books, 1992.

*Trumbore, Cindy. *Discovering the Titanic*. Parsippany, NJ: Modern Curriculum Press, 1999.